EXIT
SMART

VOL. 3

EXIT SMART

VOL. 3

Spotlights on Leading Exit Planning Advisors

LEADING EXIT PLANNING ADVISORS

FEATURING

Kiley Peters

David Lupberger

H.B. Pasley

Vinil Ramchandran

Will Stafford

Tom Poltersdorf Jr.

Mike Sedlak

Jayne McQuillan

Joy Randels

Linda Ruffenach

Exit Smart Vol. 3/ Mark Imperial —1st ed.

Chief Editor/ Shannon Buritz

ISBN: 978-1-954757-27-1

Remarkable Press™

Royalties from the retail sales of **"EXIT SMART Vol 3: Spotlights on Leading Exit Planning Advisors"** are donated to the Global Autism Project:

AUTISM KNOWS **NO BORDERS;**
FORTUNATELY NEITHER DO WE.®

The Global Autism Project 501(C)3 is a nonprofit organization that provides training to local individuals in evidence-based practice for individuals with autism.

The Global Autism Project believes that every child has the ability to learn, and their potential should not be limited by geographical bounds.

The Global Autism Project seeks to eliminate the disparity in service provision seen around the world by providing high-quality training to individuals providing services in their local community. This training is made sustainable through regular training trips and contiguous remote training.

You can learn more about the Global Autism Project and make direct donations by visiting **GlobalAutismProject.org.**

Contents

A Note to the Reader

Thank you for obtaining your copy of "EXIT SMART Vol. 3: Spotlights on Leading Exit Planning Advisors." This book was originally created as a series of live interviews on my business podcast; that's why it reads like a series of conversations, rather than a traditional book that talks at you.

My team and I have personally invited these professionals to share their knowledge because they have demonstrated that they are true advocates for the success of their clients and have shown their great ability to educate the public on the topic of exiting businesses.

I wanted you to feel as though the participants and I are talking with you, much like a close friend or relative, and felt that creating the material this way would make it easier for you to grasp the topics and put them to use quickly, rather than wading through hundreds of pages.

So relax, grab a pen and paper, take notes, and get ready to learn some fascinating insights from our Leading Exit Planning Advisors.

Warmest regards,

Mark Imperial

Publisher, Author, and Radio Personality

Introduction

"**EXIT SMART Vol. 3: Spotlights on Leading Exit Planning Advisors**" is a collaborative book series featuring leading professionals from across the country.

Remarkable Press™ would like to extend a heartfelt thank you to all participants who took the time to submit their chapter and offer their support in becoming ambassadors for this project.

100% of the royalties from this book's retail sales will be donated to the Global Autism Project. Should you want to make a direct donation, visit their website at **GlobalAutismProject.org**

KILEY PETERS

KILEY PETERS

CONVERSATION WITH KILEY PETERS

Kiley, you are the founder of RAYNE IX. Tell us
about your work and the people you help.

$$\cdots \text{———} \underset{\text{⊼}}{\text{———}} \cdots$$

Kiley Peters: I work with professional service-based women small business owners. My work is primarily helping them understand what success looks like to them because it's a very personal journey. I help women business owners define success for themselves and craft a business strategy that maps out how to make their dreams a reality. That may include exiting their business, partnering, scaling up or down, or liquidating, depending on each owner's unique situation.

What do women business owners tend
to need the most help with?

---✦---

Kiley Peters: Specifically with women business owners, I find there is a lot of pressure to scale because that's the big, sexy thing to do, right? Scale, scale, scale, and then someday, sell your business. But as we know, unfortunately, only 30% of businesses that go to market actually sell. And unfortunately, not many owners have been thrilled with their exit up to this point. So owners need to know what their options are. Scaling is not necessarily the best solution for everyone.

Business owners put a lot of pressure on themselves in all areas of life, especially regarding growing the business. It's nice to sit down with them and ask, "What are your goals as a human being? What do you want out of life? How much money do you need to make for that to happen? What are the ways we can leverage your business to make that happen?" It might be an exit or a sale, but you might surprise yourself and be able to build a really lucrative lifestyle business and someday call it quits. Anything is possible.

Are there common pitfalls business owners encounter during exit planning?

Kiley Peters: It will sound cliché and repetitive, but a big issue is business owners not knowing what they want. We're launching a study on this topic with women business owners. I often sit with them and ask, "What do you want?" They either get emotional or are in utter shock because nobody has ever asked them that before. As owners, they spend so much of their lives building the business but don't necessarily have a clear direction about where they are going, why they are going there, and what they want out of it.

So my advice to business owners is to take the time to figure out what success means to you. Don't think about "keeping up with the Jones." Think about you, your family, your lifestyle, and your expenses. What does that all look like for you? Once you define success for yourself, team up with a badass tax strategist who can make sure that you aren't throwing away money unnecessarily.

*Can you give us a 10,000-foot view
of your work with clients?*

Kiley Peters: I'm a consultant, a strategist, and a coach. I also focus a lot on operational efficiency. When I first meet a client, I ask, "What do you want? Let's start there. What do you want as a human being for you and your family?" That's what I call "defining owner success." Once we get really clear on that, we go into aligning business success, which is where we dive into business strategy. If you haven't already figured out your mission, vision, and values, we do that work. We also focus on who your audience is and what your key marketing messages are. In addition, we go through productizing your services because it's challenging to manage a business without pulling your hair out if you are customizing every deliverable you offer.

Then we move on to adjusted gross income (AGI) calculations to ensure you hit your profit margins. We go through financial projections, where I get really excited and geek out, and my clients say, "Thank God somebody is excited about doing this." We put together a personal and professional roadmap that serves as a game plan to make everything you want a reality. We do all this in "The D+A of Success" Workshop Series.

Additionally, we offer branding services if that is of interest to the client, along with an operational infrastructure implementation via our Operational Freedom Roadmap. In my experience, many owners have pieced solutions together and are not leveraging technology to their most significant advantage. They can save so much time by doing this, and time is the one thing we never get back. I've been running a service-based organization for the last six years, and I feel like I've gone through the trenches. I've spent thousands of dollars and hours trying to find the right solutions for this specific type of business. So we can help our clients with those strategies as well.

We have some opportunities for ongoing engagements, strategy sessions, or business support. Ultimately, it's my goal to help as many women business owners crush it as possible. I want to help them make the most money possible while living their best lives. Whatever I can do to make that happen is where my focus is.

Kiley, what inspired you to get started in this field?

Kiley Peters: I'll give you the CliffsNotes version. I started a digital marketing agency six years ago and loved the work. I have been a digital marketer by trade for the last 15+ years. A couple of years ago, a client reached out to me and said, "I want to exit my business. Can you help me with that?" I said, "I want to be very clear. I have no experience doing that, but it sounds fascinating. I will learn everything I can if you're okay with that." And she replied, "Yeah, great!"

So that led me to the Exit Planning Institute (EPI), where I became a CEPA (Certified Exit Planning Advisor) and started working with EPI on a consulting basis to help them grow their marketing team, which is just killing it right now. Over the last several years, I fell in love with and realized I excel at business strategy and operational infrastructure. Many business owners have reached out to me and asked, "How are you doing this? What you do is way over my head. I don't want to do any of this stuff." But this is the stuff I geek out on.

In 2021, I launched RAYNE IX as an executive consultancy to help small business owners because, in my opinion, they are what keep the economy going. But I encourage everyone to operate in their Zone of Genius. Often, small business owners wear a million hats, and in doing so, they're not honoring their greatest opportunity to contribute to the world. So my goal is to help business owners, specifically women business owners, identify their Zone of Genius and live in that zone.

Then I'm happy to help them organize all the moving pieces to help their business succeed and run smoothly.

Is there anything else you would like to share with business owners considering an exit?

Kiley Peters: I'd just reiterate these two things: define success for yourself and leverage technology. Put your blinders on when it comes to comparing yourself to everyone else. I do a series of workshops called "The D+A of Success," which stands for the definition and alignment of success. I currently work one-on-one with owners, but starting in the fall, we will be doing quarterly group workshops throughout the country. Check that out if it interests you. I really just want to help women business owners live their best lives.

How can people find you, connect with you, and learn more?

Kiley Peters: You can find me at KileyPeters.com or RAYNEIX. com. You can also reach me by email at kiley@rayneix.com. I am on LinkedIn and Instagram as Kiley Peters. Feel free to check out my podcast, "Welcome to Eloma."

KILEY PETERS, MBA, CEPA

FOUNDER + SMALL BUSINESS STRATEGIST
RAYNE IX

Kiley Peters is a serial entrepreneur, small business strategist, executive coach, operations consultant, and brand marketer with nearly 15 years of industry experience. She is on a mission to help 1 million women build more financially free and fulfilling lives.

She is the Founder of Brainchild Studios®, an international award-winning audience research and digital content strategy agency. She founded RAYNE IX, an executive consultancy helping professional service-based women small business owners leverage their businesses to achieve financial freedom and build fulfilling lives. She built The Starter Kit, a series of online courses guiding emerging entrepreneurs through the steps of starting a virtual business. And in 2022, she launched her podcast, Welcome to Eloma, a podcast for visionaries, entrepreneurs, and business owners who want to become better leaders, people, and pioneers.

In 2018, Brainchild Studios won the Wisconsin Marketplace Governor's Rising Star Award for a Women-Owned Business. In 2019 and 2020, Brainchild Studios was awarded international recognition as Business Services Company of the Year for a company with fewer than ten employees by the Stevie Awards.

Additionally, she has spoken across the country on the topics of entrepreneurship, small business strategy, digital content strategy, and consumer behavior research at the Exit Planning Summit, KNOW Women Summit, Content Marketing Conference, Content Marketing World, The Second City, Google, FUND Conference, Women's Entrepreneurship

Week, Milwaukee Startup Week, Local First's When Women Lead among many others.

She is a Faculty Member at Exit Planning Institute (EPI), an Adjunct Professor at Marquette University teaching Digital Content Strategy, and holds dual Bachelor of Arts degrees from Marquette University and an MBA from the University of Illinois at Chicago. She is also a mentor at BizStarts and Wisconsin Women's Business Initiative Corporation (WWBIC).

EMAIL:
kiley@rayneix.com

WEBSITE:
RAYNEIX.com

OTHER:
WelcomeToEloma.com, KileyPeters.com

DAVID
LUPBERGER

DAVID LUPBERGER

Conversation With David Lupberger

David, you are the founder of Contractor Exit Strategy.
Tell us about your work and the people you help.

---✦---

David Lupberger: I was a building contractor for 25 years. As I approached my 60s, I asked myself, "What's next?" When I did public presentations, I discovered that half of the room had white or no hair. My struggle was concurrent with their concerns, "What's next? Where do I go from here?" So I began having conversations with people about what their next phase of work looked like. Interestingly, most didn't want to quit, but they wanted to shift their focus from day-to-day activities and functions. So we began talking about a process to make that happen. I opened Contractor Exit Strategy to guide owners through the process in a systematic fashion, so the company maintains value, saves time, and each owner can do what they do best.

How much thought do business owners put
into transitioning to the next phase?

--- ⟱ ---

David Lupberger: They really don't put any thought into it. The market has been so strong for the past 10 to 12 years. I sit down with owners and ask, "Are you planning for any transition or exit? And more importantly, are you planning for business continuity? What if something happened to you or a family member, forcing you to be unable to work for four to eight weeks?" 90% of these companies would close because the owner carries all the weight of company management and ongoing functions. So we have some really wonderful conversations about the owner's role in the company and how to hand off some of that responsibility systematically. It does take time. It can easily take three years or longer. So it's essential to start thinking about it as soon as possible. Ultimately, you will leave your business. So please don't do it haphazardly; do it with a plan.

Are there common myths or misconceptions
about exiting a business?

--- ⟱ ---

David Lupberger: The interesting part is that many owners I talk to say they would like to work less. Then I'll have questions, "What would you be doing with that extra free time?" Often, the initial reaction is, "I will play golf." Well, guess what? You're not going to play golf more than three days a week. So after about three months, you are going to be pretty bored.

Secondly, I've had people say, "I just want to sell my business and go sell sandwiches." Again, in three months, you would be bored to tears. You're in this business because it's vital. It's creative. Every day is different. You manage people, and you affect people's lives, both your clients and your employees. There's a vitality here, so let's maintain that vitality.

But like I said, "What's the roadmap? Where are you going?" A past survey revealed that 80% of business owners regretted the sale of their business a year later. The primary reason was they had not reassigned that passion and thought, "If I'm moving out of doing this, what am I moving into?" I've discovered with the contractors I'm working with that they don't want to retire. They would just love to move away from some of these day-to-day responsibilities, hand them off to good employees, and go from working 60 hours a week to 25. And it can be done. But it's a roadmap, and it needs to be planned.

Can you give us a 10,000-foot view of the
services you provide your clients?

--- ⟰ ---

David Lupberger: I have several surveys to understand what you are doing now. One of these is called an "Owner-Centricity Quiz." What are all of the functions you are involved with? What are you doing right now? What do you *need* to do? The answers help us prioritize these items.

Secondly, I introduce a "Management Succession Worksheet." If you're going to delegate these things, who are you delegating them to? In what order? And then lastly, what's the process for delegating those things? I'm a firm advocate for putting everything in writing. If you put it in writing, there's no gray area. So I have pre-written job descriptions I can share with people, all in a Word format. They can be modified according to the company's functions. The reality is that you can do this. But you can do it much more quickly and efficiently by working with someone like me.

David, what inspired you to get started in this field?

--- ⟰ ---

David Lupberger: It was really my age. I hit 60, and I had been consulting with contractors. And then suddenly, I wanted to know what was next for me. I had my head down for 30 years, raising a child with my wife, and as an empty nester, I began to look up and say, "What do I want to do?" Business can be so all-consuming, and it's easy to get caught up in the "right now." So these conversations are so important to have with my clients. Sometimes I come across someone really interested when they first started the company, and six months later, they're not. So it's about putting together a realistic plan and understanding that, similar to a construction project, it is subject to change.

Is there anything else you would like to share with business owners considering an exit?

⁎

David Lupberger: Michael Gerber wrote a book, "The E-Myth." It's helping people systemize moving out of some of these day-to-day operations. He was once asked, "What do you see in the most successful companies?" He said, "They built their companies with the end in mind."

I want to have that same conversation. You will not be here forever. You don't need to work 60 hours a week. What can we do to take your unique skill set and empower people in the company to continue generating income while strategically taking a role in the company that you enjoy? Build with the end in mind.

How can people find you, connect
with you, and learn more?

David Lupberger: My website is www.contractorexitstrategy.com. But don't think of it as exiting. Think of it as transitioning, creating a plan for the future.

DAVID LUPBERGER

CERTIFIED EXIT PLANNING ADVISOR
FOR THE CONSTRUCTION INDUSTRY
CONTRACTOR EXIT STRATEGY

David Lupberger has been involved with custom home building and remodeling for over 30 years. After moving to the Washington DC area in 1988, he practiced high-end residential remodeling and focused on delivering the highest quality service to his clients. Over 90 percent of his work came from repeat and referral business, demonstrating the trust he developed with clients.

That experience in managing customer expectations led him to write a book entitled "Managing the Emotional Homeowner," which has become one of the bibles of the remodeling industry and helped hundreds of remodelers improve the level of service they provide clients.

Lupberger believes fervently that the best customer service only comes when a remodeler can deliver consistent results, which happens only with proven systems. He spent four years writing the "Remodelers Turnkey Program." This series of manuals is a basic how-to text on running a remodeling company. He recently authored " The Home Asset Management Plan," a business system showing contractors how to implement a "client for life" program with their homeowner clients.

From his base in Boulder, Colorado, he now consults with both Remodelers and industry manufacturers such as General Electric to maximize customer service relationships between all the industry partners. He travels extensively, speaking to thousands of remodelers across the country, and is a regular on the seminar series at national trade shows. He also is a columnist for numerous industry trade magazines.

EMAIL:
David@DavidLupberger.com

PHONE:
303-442-3702

WEBSITE:
www.ContractorExitStrategy.com

OTHER:
www.RemodelForce.com

H.B. PASLEY

H.B. PASLEY

CONVERSATION WITH H.B. PASLEY

H.B., you are the founder of Ideal Client Experience and Graceful Exit Planning. Tell us about your work and the people you help.

--- ⚑ ---

H.B. Pasley: I've been a coach my entire life. When I was only 16 years old, I earned my lifeguard certification. I thought it would be cool to be a lifeguard, sit in the tall chair, and spin the whistle on my finger. However, I discovered that I was even better at teaching swimming lessons. (This is probably because I failed beginning swimming lessons four times in a row. I was empathetic to the situation!)

After four decades of working in creative communication, I've published many books and songs and been on thousands of stages. I learned the art of leading a team, focusing messaging, and just getting things done. Event work is very much about getting things done on time. It is also about building long-term, trusting relationships with key leaders. So today, I leverage all of that collected experience by working with business owners who are usually hitting their heads on growth problems. Growth problems, by the way, are the dead center of transition planning problems.

I would add that the leaders I work with are the kind of business owners who need to take care of people. They know that client care is job number one, whether their client experience is five minutes long or five years long. My specialty is developing leaders' Relational IQ and then building their Process IQ so they can grow with better and better clients over time. My advisory clients all receive fundamental coaching toward smart exit planning. This is because you can't exit well if your business is not growing, and growth should be fundamental to any business strategy. To put it another way: it is a nightmare to try and make any kind of transition if your business is not strong and growing.

*How much thought do business owners
put into exit planning?*

--- ↟ ---

H.B. Pasley: Tragically, exit planning is often deferred until a crisis moment when an owner has to pull back or sell their business under duress. It's like calling the emergency room and paying big money for a healthcare problem you could have solved a little at a time along the way. I wish it weren't the case. I do find that there are many thoughtful business owners, but these same business owners really should be asking themselves, "What will make my business more valuable over time?" This is a seriously relevant question regardless of your location on the business life cycle.

Business owners who are 35 or 45 don't want to talk about exiting because they think of it as an end-of-life campaign. But if you ask them, "Would you like to build value within your business so that as it grows over time, it becomes more valuable in the marketplace?" most will say, "Yes!" Since I work with service professionals, this is a very important question because they're not always accumulating assets or manufactured inventory. They don't make widgets; they are the widget. So this conversation is incredibly potent for service professionals. I believe you have to start early in your understanding of the basic principles, and then you won't be caught off guard when it's your time.

Can you give us a 10,000-foot view of
what it looks like to work with you?

———✦———

H.B. Pasley: At one level, exit planning or building value is just an algebra formula: EBITDA times your MULTIPLE (the X). One part of the algebra is simply measuring your cash flow and assets on hand. This is the tangible value stuff that your accountant could help you discover. So that's one thing in the algebra equation. The other part of the equation is this mysterious X. It's the multiplier that people talk about. I concentrate on helping business owners understand this X. If we were talking about the value of your home, then the X is the kind of stuff that makes your home attractive, not just the basic land valuation the real estate guy gives. Does it have a view? Is it clean? Does it feel inviting? Is it laid out well? This is all of the functional stuff.

It works the same way for a business. There's much more than just the basic cash value in your financials. When a future buyer looks at your business, they naturally ask questions about the functional stuff of your business: Do you have a team that can sustain the work when you're not there anymore? Do you have a process so easy to follow that we could take your team out and put a new team in, and they could still do the job? And then finally, do you have a purpose so clear that your location in the marketplace is easy to spot and your customer base can easily find you?

So there are more ways to improve the X, but my point is that many business owners don't even realize they can improve the X! This is important because, in this basic algebra, multiplication is way more powerful than addition. You can add to your asset mix, but you affect a much more significant increase in your company's value by boosting your multiplier. This is where people should be asking, "How do we do it, H.B.?" Here is the answer. Getting people, processes, and purpose to start working together is key.

My primary role is coaching those high-level ideas to ensure business owners set important annual goals in all three areas. This is often a work of the heart before it is just a technical implementation. So I'm much less of a technician in my particular coaching function than a heart coach. Whether a business owner is early or late in their development, it is helpful to ask, "What do you want out of this business right now?" There are all kinds of answers to that question. And then I might ask, "What do you want from the business ten years from now? What if you don't sell in ten years but want to transition to only part-time?" These kinds of questions can help people solve the big stuff before they go out and hire the expensive technicians, the valuation experts, or the people who get into the nitty gritty business of taking them to market.

It sounds like exit planning should occur when you start your business. Can you speak to that?

--- ——————⬧—————— ---

H.B. Pasley: It should start right away. In fact, there's no such thing as business planning without the idea of increasing value, which means business planning always has exit planning embedded. People just don't always know what to call it. When working with clients, I often say, "Before it is anything else, exit planning is a matter of the heart." People leading businesses must know that they're in charge of how that business grows; healthy, unhealthy, fast, or slow. They also get to decide how much they want it to be worth. They are also in charge of how well their team can function without them both now and in the future. All of these things are determined early in a business plan. They really can't be solved well at the last minute.

H.B., how did you go from teaching swimming lessons to exit planning? What inspired you to get started in this field?

---⚡---

H.B. Pasley: I'm new to the arena of exit planning and formal business coaching. I have almost four decades of experience in publishing and nonprofit leadership. I got involved with financial advisory services about three or four years ago. It was a natural evolution of my desire to coach others' success. One of the firms I began to work with did a lot of transition planning. I was the leader of strategic development for the firm. I would sit around the table with business owners and listen to the financial advisory team start to help them think through the issues: What do you want to keep? What do you want to leave? How will it affect the team? How will it affect your spouse? How does this affect your personal financial situation? I realized that it was such a tender heart issue. The owners definitely needed technical answers, but they were struggling with heart-level questions that would help them make better strategic decisions. These were very deep and personal questions for them. My four decades of working as a consultant, counselor, and coach may have helped me under-stand the situation better than some of the financial nerds I worked with. So I became interested in transition planning to help adults make some adult decisions while getting some high Relational IQ added in. I was afraid many people would go into exit planning thinking they could just hire three engineering specialists and get everything they needed. I took a different approach. I thought, "Well, I know those engineers (and they're really, really smart people), but I would like to help you with some of the bigger picture and heart-level stuff, so you're more confident in the whole process. Let's get you driving the bus; then you will know what kind of engineers to take with you."

Is there anything else you would like to share?

H.B. Pasley: Any business owner considering exit planning *could* go and Google information on exit planning. They could easily find a few books and resources on the topic. However, I find that knowledge is easy to get nowadays, but wisdom is not. So, I'm always trying to encourage people to make a personal connection when they want to solve a problem. The wisdom you need to safely navigate the idea of transition planning or growing your business is probably embodied in a person. If you've never hired a business consultant, an advisor, or a professional coach, this might be your time. After all, it's not a permanent thing. It's just a season of engaging somebody who might look at your challenges from a different angle. Some very wise people are included in this book on learning to *Exit Smart.* I bet each of them could help you process your decision-making in ways you never thought of. That's the power of reaching out to a third-party perspective partner. I believe this is the best way for people to start thinking about exit planning or growing their business: *hire a guide.* Ask this question, "Who can I build a relationship with for a season? Who will help me think better, get more strategic, and make good decisions moving forward?"

How can people find you, connect with you, and learn more?

H.B. Pasley: I operate my primary coaching and advisory program at www.idealclientexperience.com. As you can tell by the name, I focus on helping business owners discover their ideal clients and how to create such an excellent experience for those clients that they become client advocates over time. I have also created an easy way for owners who want to zero in on transition planning at my website: www.gracefulexit-planning.com. Some of my clients are primarily concerned with growth problems. For them, I weave value-building into the basics of our strategy work together. Some are older and are staring down transition problems. And some of my exit planning clients have already made their financial transition but are now working on how to move gracefully into an exciting and valuable second half. On either website, you can find some information about me, and it is super easy to set up a free 30-minute consultation as soon as you would like. I offer these initial conversations for free because I think everyone deserves a listening ear when they feel stuck. I remember the scary part of swimming lessons was the moment you realized you were in over your head. When we are in the deep end of the pool, and we are in over our heads–this is the time we really need someone to reach out and help. It is my joy to help, so I offer these first conversations freely without reservation.

H.B. PASLEY, GROWTH ADVOCATE℠, CEPA

FOUNDER
IDEAL CLIENT EXPERIENCE
& GRACEFUL EXIT PLANNING

H.B. Pasley serves as a Growth Advocate℠ for business leaders. He is an expert at helping people-first owners who are hitting their heads on growth problems. H.B. has been a coach, a creative, and a professional communicator for nearly four decades. He has published many books and countless leadership guides, facilitated thousands of people in leadership development retreats, and produced over 7 million song streams on Spotify. Even after all that, he is fond of deflecting attention from his accomplishments by saying, "My real claim to fame is that I have failed at more ventures than most will ever attempt ... and I took a lot of notes."

H.B. is a founder and chief executive by nature. He has founded works in tech, financial services, charitable orgs, and in the arts. He founded and presided over an arts-focused Christian nonprofit that served the marginalized for two decades. His DNA is to start things; however, it may be his lifelong work with very strong, very talented people that uniquely equips him to be a professional advisor. He says it was "in the school of hard knocks" where he gleaned his best wisdom for helping others. Refreshingly, H.B. openly speaks of his own failures as some of his greatest learning moments. As a business coach, he often refers to himself as a "perspective partner."

Presently, H.B. lives in Colorado Springs, Colorado, with his wife, Robin, an award-winning interior designer. His two sons live in Phoenix, Arizona. Xander is a student at Grand Canyon University, and Zane recently graduated with a degree in Entrepreneurial Business. H.B. loves golf though he is bad at it. He is better at fly fishing, reading books, and hiking. He loves to be on the water.

EMAIL:

hbpasley@idealclientexperience.com

PHONE:

719-633-2515

WEBSITE:

www.idealclientexperience.com

OTHER:

www.gracefulexitplanning.com

VINIL
RAMCHANDRAN

VINIL RAMCHANDRAN
CONVERSATION WITH VINIL RAMCHANDRAN

Vinil, you are the founder of Dream Business Brokers.
Tell us about your work and the people you help.

--- ⚹ ---

Vinil Ramchandran: At Dream Business Brokers, we work with business owners looking to exit their companies. Most of our clients are approaching retirement age and want to pass on their legacy to someone else who will take the business to the next level while continuing to take great care of their employees and customers. We work with privately owned companies, primarily in California. Occasionally, we work in other areas but tend to keep pretty busy just in our own backyard. Many of our clients are in the manufacturing and distribution space, although we work with other sectors, such as B2B services and tech companies. I always say an informed seller and an informed buyer make the best clients because they know what they're getting into and have realistic expectations. So, a lot of my work involves educating clients on the process of preparing and selling a business.

Are there preconceived notions about exiting a business?

Vinil Ramchandran: It's common for business owners not to think about what's next. They have a thought in the back of their minds about exiting someday, but they haven't formalized it with a documented plan. So that's where we come in. It's ideal when a client knows exactly what they want and is ready to package the business and sell it because that's most of what we do. We package the business, take it to market, find the ideal buyer, and act as a matchmaker to help the buyer and seller achieve their objectives.

That said, business owners have typically not put a lot of thought into this and do not have a plan. With exit planning, we meet with sellers a few years before they are ready to pull the trigger. We help value the business, identify where they are and what's important to them, and devise a plan to bridge the gap between where the business is today and where they want it to be when they exit to make their dreams a reality.

Can you give us a 10,000-foot view
of the exit planning process?

---✖---

Vinil Ramchandran: This is a team sport. There is not one single person who can handle everything that goes into exit planning. A lot of our exit planning work is complimentary. We offer this as a value-added service for sellers seeking our assistance selling their business. Ultimately, we want each client to have a better exit when the time comes.

The process starts with meeting the client and understanding their needs. What do they have? What does the business look like today? Is it ready to take to market? What can be done to clean up the business and improve performance to prepare it for the market down the road? What are the seller's expectations? It's common for sellers to have an inflated expectation of value, thinking the business is worth more than it really is. And that's part of the education process. We evaluate the business to help them understand the market value and how that compares to what they want to get out of it.

Meanwhile, if needed, we bring in other team members, including financial planners, accountants, attorneys, and other business improvement consultants. The seller may need to be advised on the tax consequences of the sale, streamline their contracts, and do some estate planning. Once their ducks are in a row, and they're clear on what they want to do and the timeline, we get involved with the heavy lifting. Depending on the state of the business, they may have to work on several value drivers to help improve the valuation. You can't just ask for what you want and expect the market to pay it; you must work on building value.

Are there common pitfalls owners
face when exiting a business?

Vinil Ramchandran: A big one is the lack of preparation. We talk to many owners in their late 70s who want to get out now but haven't done any preparation. Another common one involves books and records. Many small business owners are working with very informal bookkeeping practices. Sometimes the documentation is not very good, it's not very clean, and there are a lot of personal expenses running through the business. We can work through a lot of that, but sometimes there are issues of substantial dollars and cents running through the business that cannot be reasonably adjusted. A lender will not look at it and say, "Hey, we'll trust that is a personal expense." So you do need a little bit of time to clean things up. Owners need to think ahead and consult with a professional, whether an exit planner, a CPA, or a business intermediary like myself, to clean up their books well before pulling the trigger and selling the business.

Vinil, what inspired you to get started in this field?

--- ⚶ ---

Vinil Ramchandran: I got out of corporate America about 10 or 11 years ago and looked at acquiring a business myself. Through the process of working with many different intermediaries, I noticed a gap. It was clear that many were only working on a transactional level, without really going deeper, understanding what was important to the buyer and the seller, and trying to bridge that gap. I just knew there was a ton of opportunity there. I started as a business consultant and worked with many companies; my background has been industrial engineering and corporate management for many years. So I had a good perspective and solid understanding of the operational side regarding how a business runs and where the pitfalls and opportunities are. I just knew I could do a better job adding value to sellers looking to exit. So it's something that I enjoy and am very passionate about. There's a lot of opportunity as business owners continue to exit at a feverish pace. Many baby boomers are retiring, so this market will grow as the need increases over the next several years. And I'm here to help.

Is there anything else you would like to share
with business owners considering an exit?

---✦---

Vinil Ramchandran: Understand the timeline of when you are going to exit. One of the issues is something we refer to as the "Dismal Ds." These include death, disease, divorce, disability, declining sales, dissension between partnerships, and more. These factors can force a business owner to sell. Selling out of desperation is the worst time to sell because buyers can "smell it" and will often take advantage of the situation. It's crucial to avoid these circumstances by planning in advance and exiting while things are going well and you are in control.

How can people find you, connect
with you, and learn more?

---✦---

Vinil Ramchandran: You can reach me on my website: www.dreambusinessbrokers.com. My email is vinil@dreambusinessbrokers.com. You can also simply give us a call at 562-761-4689.

VINIL RAMCHANDRAN, CM&AP, CBB, CBI, CEPA

FOUNDER
DREAM BUSINESS BROKERS

Vinil Ramchandran, Founder of Dream Business Brokers, is a Certified Business Intermediary. He brings over 20 years of business experience to help his clients maximize the value of their businesses as they prepare for an exit. He is passionate about his work and has built a reputation for being a results-oriented business broker who has successfully closed numerous challenging transactions.

His professional experience ranges from working in corporate America as an Industrial Engineer, Plant Manager, Service Manager, & General Manager to small business ownership and business brokerage in various sectors, including manufacturing, service, tech, and more! This experience has given him a broad business perspective with a unique mix of operational knowledge, negotiation skills, and marketing savvy!

EMAIL:
Vinil@DreamBusinessBrokers.com

PHONE:
562-761-4689

WEBSITE:
www.DreamBusinessBrokers.com

WILL
STAFFORD

Conversation With Will Stafford

Will, you are the Managing Attorney of Stafford Law Firm. Tell us about your work and the people you help.

---✣---

Will Stafford: We are an estate planning and business law firm in Houston, Texas. We specialize in helping families and businesses at the intersection of those practice areas. We enjoy working with families who own small and medium-sized businesses in Texas and around the country. One of the most important things to know and understand is that exit planning is estate planning, and estate planning is exit planning when you're a small business owner. So we walk the divide between those practice areas and ensure that our clients are prepared for an eventual exit from their business because it's coming one way or another.

How much thought do business owners put into exit planning? Do they even know where to start?

———————✦———————

Will Stafford: Unfortunately, the answer is almost always none, and they don't know where to start. My initial conversation with business owners usually goes like this: "What's your plan when you no longer want to work in your business?" I typically get answers like "I don't know" or "My kids will take it over." Very rarely do they have an actual plan already in mind or in place. "I don't know" is an easy place to start. "My kids will take it over" is a little more difficult because the follow-up question is, "Do your kids even want to take it over?" And the answer to that question is almost always, "I don't know."

Can you give us a 10,000-foot view of the exit planning process? What does it look like to work with you?

———————✦———————

Will Stafford: We want to start conversations about exit planning years before any potential exit. Four, five, or even six years ahead of time is optimal. At that point, we bring in a team of professionals, including myself as the attorney, financial advisors, accountants, and insurance professionals. We start looking at all of the pieces of the business that we can improve to make the future exit more feasible and financially profitable.

From a legal perspective, we ask questions such as, "Do you have a risk management program in place? Is it robust and functional? Do you have an estate plan in place for you personally and for the business? How would the business continue running if something happened to you unexpectedly? Do you have a partner in it? Do you have a buy/sell agreement? If so, how is it funded?"

When planning for an unexpected business succession, most business owners first consider a buy/sell agreement. But they don't generally take it a step further to have it funded. It's all well and good to have an agreement that says, "My partner is going to buy out my family if I were to get hit by a truck." But the agreement is not super useful if the partner doesn't have the $5 million to buy out your family when the truck actually hits you. So we think about all those issues up front and ensure that we plan for unexpected eventualities. Then we can start looking five years down the road and plan intentionally for a smooth exit.

Are there common myths and misconceptions
about selling a business?

Will Stafford: People always come to us and say, "I'm ready to retire; I want to sell my business." And we say, "Sure. When would you like to sell?" They say, "As soon as possible." We can certainly go ahead and start a process to try to sell the business immediately. However, the problem is that you're never going to maximize the value you could have realized if we had some lead time to make the business more attractive to a buyer. And when you're talking about making a business more attractive to a buyer, you're really talking about two factors. The first one is quantitative factors: money. How much money does the business make? You also have qualitative factors, which are the parts of the business that aren't necessarily showing up on the balance sheet. Does the business rely on the owner for revenue? Does it have systemized processes and procedures to run without the key decision maker involved daily? Does it have a distributed customer base? Or does it rely on one or two major customers for all of its business?

We can change these things with some lead time to make the business more valuable. These items can materially increase the multiple paid on the business' revenue, which is actually the most impactful way to increase the value of the business.

Will, what inspired you to get started in this field?

--- ————————— ⚓ ————————— ---

Will Stafford: I spent the first decade of my career as a traditional corporate attorney, doing large corporate transactions, mergers and acquisitions, and securities offerings. A few years ago, I was working for a private firm, and that firm did a lot of estate planning for families, while I did a lot of planning for businesses. Because of that intersection, I got pulled into many cases that walked the line between the two. And that's when I really started to conceptualize the practice that I have today because it's this amazing hybrid practice that puts together all of my experience from the corporate world and all of the things I love about helping families and small business owners plan for their futures. It's such a rewarding area to practice in. A business owner may be the most incredible widget maker on Earth, but comprehensive exit and estate planning are not something they can do for themselves. I enjoy stepping in and giving them the gift of a plan, whether it will be implemented six months or six years from now. It takes a massive weight off their shoulders to know that plan exists.

Is there anything else you would like to share with business owners considering an exit?

---⋏---

Will Stafford: One thing I would like to reiterate is to start early if you think there is a chance that you may one day want to sell your business or exit in any way. An exit doesn't always mean a sale. It can mean a succession to your children, purposefully while alive or after death. It can mean letting a partner take over or letting your employees take over by setting up an ESOP. But the process of determining the best exit option takes time. So the earlier you come to us, the better because we can not only help you find the right path but have enough time to make that path impactful to the value of the business.

How can people find you, connect with you, and learn more?

Will Stafford: Our website is www.staffordlawtx.com. You can email me directly at will@staffordlawtx.com or call us at 713-929-9992.

This book does not create an attorney-client relationship, and nothing in this book should be construed to create such a relationship or taken as legal advice. An attorney-client relationship can only be created pursuant to a written agreement with our firm.

WILL STAFFORD, ESQ., CEPA

MANAGING ATTORNEY
STAFFORD LAW FIRM

Planning for your life or business is no easy task. While you might understand where you are going (or where you want to go), the right path isn't always obvious. That's where I come in. I help individuals, families, and business owners take the right steps toward securing their legacy and protecting their families from the "unknowns" of tomorrow.

My name is Will Stafford, and I created Stafford Law Firm to make sure that business owners like you have a plan in place to seamlessly transition your legacy to the next stage of life, whatever that may be for you. My firm was the result of years of frustration with traditional law firms and their estate planning processes that don't align with the long terms goals of their business owner clients. The relationships were transactional, not relational, in nature. And after I had a personal experience where I was directly affected by another firm's transactional planning, enough was enough.

My mission is to make sure that every family and small business owner has the tools and knowledge at hand to make educated and empowered decisions for themselves and their loved ones.

EMAIL:
will@staffordlawtx.com

PHONE:
713-929-9992

WEBSITE:
www.staffordlawtx.com

TOM
POLTERSDORF JR.

TOM POLTERSDORF JR.
CONVERSATION WITH TOM POLTERSDORF JR.

Tom, you are the founder of Beyond Your Exit Wealth Management. Tell us about your work and the people you help.

---✦---

Tom Poltersdorf Jr.: I'm a financial planner and business coach. My niche is small business owners with revenues between one and ten million looking to exit within the next five to seven years. One of their core values is time; they want to work smarter, not harder. They are looking for a work/life balance to spend more time with family, enjoy hobbies, and travel.

How much thought do business owners
put into exit planning?

———★———

Tom Poltersdorf Jr.: There is not a lot of thought that goes into it. Many business owners think a magical buyer will appear when they are ready to exit, sell, or transition. That's not the case. Some crazy statistics from the Exit Planning Institute indicate that 80% of businesses that go to market never sell. 75% of business owners who sell end up regretting the decision because they didn't get the value they hoped for or needed. Our mission is to lead with education on these topics and spread the word on what works to prevent owners from becoming a statistic.

Can you give us a 10,000-foot view of
what it looks like to work with you?

———★———

Tom Poltersdorf Jr.: I put a lot of thought into the process when I started my firm, hence the name, Beyond Your Exit Wealth Management. So the focus begins with the vision. What are you going to do once you exit your business? Again, statistics show that owners regret selling because they don't know what to do with themselves after the sale. So we help create a roadmap for where you want to be five years or less down the road. Exit planning is simply building a strategy for how you would like to leave your business ideally and finding out if your business is attractive to sell. The majority of businesses are not attractive. The exit planning process helps make your business more valuable by becoming more efficient in building processes and having the right people in place. The goal is to make your business more valuable year after year until you have the option to sell. The funny thing is, we often get these businesses up and running so efficiently that the owner doesn't want to sell because the business is no longer running through them 100%. That's the ideal space we'd like to get to through exit planning.

Are there common pitfalls owners face when it comes to exit planning?

Tom Poltersdorf Jr.: One of the most significant issues is an owner who is ready to retire, but the entire business runs through them. The business owner is the epicenter of the business. They are the leading sales guy; they know their customers and have built all the relationships. So if you remove the owner, the relationships are lost, and the business becomes unattractive. Just like myself, most business owners like to be in control; I think we can all agree on that. But to make the business attractive for sale, you have to delegate more, build systems and processes, and train someone else to be the lead salesperson to get as much off your plate as possible. You want to get to a point where you could take a three to six-month vacation, and the business would still grow in your absence. That's an excellent spot to be in.

Is there an ideal timeframe to start planning an exit?

Tom Poltersdorf Jr.: As soon as possible. The misconception is, "Hey, I'm 65. I'm thinking about retiring in five years. I am going to start exit planning now." Remember that exit planning is simply a good business strategy. So even if you are only 40 or 45 years old, implementing exit planning *now* makes your business more profitable, drives revenue, and makes your life a whole lot easier because you don't have to be involved in the day-to-day operations. Planning with the end in mind is best. You don't want to wake up at 70 years old hoping to retire and realize that your business is not attractive or sellable to fund the next phase of your life. Start forming an exit plan as soon as possible, regardless of whether or not you have any intention to exit.

Here's another reason I want to stress this point of having an exit plan in place; 50% of exits are involuntary. That's right, involuntary. That means forced. Can you imagine being forced to exit your business? And this happens all the time because of one of the following: Death, Divorce, Disability, Distress, and Disagreement. They are all dramatic life events that can completely blindside you and force you to exit at the worst times in your life. If you want to take care of yourself and your family, and protect your business, get an exit plan in place.

Tom, what inspired you to get started in this field?

Tom Poltersdorf Jr.: I've been in the industry for over ten years. I fell in love with business owners when I started working with them one-on-one. I wanted to work with business owners differently than traditional financial services professionals, so I started my firm. And I focus on talking about the business. Many folks say, "Hey, you have to invest in a 401k; you have to be in the market." We all know that. But many business owners want to talk about the business because that's the biggest asset on their balance sheet. It's where all their net worth is. So what's cool is I can help these business owners by talking about business strategy. These conversations give people options on being able to sell their business or stay in their business and start a second business, or whatever else they want to do. So I've taken a different path to work with this clientele.

Is there anything else you would like to share with business owners considering an exit?

Tom Poltersdorf Jr.: Get an open market valuation on your business. The tricky thing about being an owner is the business is your baby. So you need an objective perspective because there is a bias when you have been growing the business for ten to twenty years or more. A third-party valuation will give you a place to start, and then you can build a roadmap from there.

How can people find you, connect with you, and learn more?

Tom Poltersdorf Jr.: We lead with education. So I have a podcast, "Business Exit Success," where you can start educating yourself on the exit planning game. My website is www. beyondyourexitwm.com. There is a "Knowledge Center" tab with many free educational articles. If you are ready for a conversation, you can book a call, and we'd be happy to chat.

TOM POLTERSDORF JR., CFP®, CEPA®

FOUNDER
BEYOND YOUR EXIT WEALTH MANAGEMENT

Tom Poltersdorf Jr. has spent over a decade in this profession, working first at Morgan Stanley, TD Ameritrade, and other investment firms in the greater Harrisburg, PA, area before deciding to launch his own firm. Ultimately, he wanted to serve and add massive value to small business owners in a much different way than the traditional financial services industry. His experience and certifications not only provide him with the expertise to advise on the personal side of financial planning but also on an owner's greatest asset: Their Business.

When he's not working with clients, he enjoys going on adventures with his wife and two kiddos. Having memorable and fun experiences with his family has always been his priority. In his downtime, he loves music. Playing the drums has been his favorite hobby since he was a kid. He also enjoys working out, reading, and listening to podcasts.

Tom is a CERTIFIED FINANCIAL PLANNER™ Professional, a Certified Exit Planning Advisor, and a Certified Value Builder™.

EMAIL:
tom@beyondyourexitwm.com

PHONE:
717-937-1612

WEBSITE:
https://beyondyourexitwm.com/

MIKE SEDLAK

CONVERSATION WITH MIKE SEDLAK

Mike, you are the founder of Golden Trail Advisers.
Tell us about your work and the people you help.

--- ❋ ---

Mike Sedlak: Every business owner reaches the point where their business becomes an asset rather than the place they work. As an investment advisor, I've received education through the Exit Planning Institute on how to best transition out of a business. So our ideal client is someone who's looking ahead because you can't wait until the last minute to sell your business and expect a good price for it. We work best with people planning for the future and thinking about what they would like to do after the business is sold.

How much thought do business owners
put into exit planning?

Mike Sedlak: Exit planning is on the back burner because business owners have nine million things going on. Exit planning doesn't bring them immediate payback. It's three to five years down the road at minimum, so it tends to get pushed down the road. I liken it to estate planning. How many of us want to sit with an attorney and spend our time on an estate plan? We know it is important to our families, but we tend to put off estate planning until something prompts us to make it a priority.

Even though business owners are busy, we try to help them see why exit planning is so important. We plug in a value for their business as a portion of their financial projection, and we have to be accurate about that, or else the financial projection will not be reliable. We must have accurate input and assumptions to create and implement a financial plan that works.

What are the pitfalls of improper planning?

Mike Sedlak: If you don't plan, you depend on luck. Many business owners think that someone will just come along and buy their business for a good price when they are ready to retire. But that rarely happens. Typically, a business owner gets bored, tired, or ill. And then, they don't have any plans and try to do everything while barely being able to keep the business going. On top of that, they need a good exit plan. But by that point, it's already too late. So the pitfall is they sell for a lower price or can't even sell at all. That is devastating to their overall financial plan. Most business owners have a high percentage of their net worth tied up in their business. The business must be thought about like a portfolio of investments that needs to be carefully and thoughtfully managed.

Can you give us a 10,000-foot view of what it looks like to work with you?

Mike Sedlak: It all starts with your goals. If you are 25 years old and just started a business, we won't emphasize retirement heavily. But you might have a goal to sell in five or six years and start another business. So we start with a plan, determine the value, and determine how that value fits into the overall plan. Everyone is taught that they need to put money into their 401K plan as a retirement resource, but we teach people they need to grow the value of their business because it's a significant asset, not just a job. If you are very wealthy, you also need to do estate planning to ensure the money goes to people you care about in a tax-efficient way.

Then we work with experts to look at things we can do to improve the value of the business before getting to the point of selling. Perhaps we need to bring in someone to help with marketing or operations.

Lastly, we want to ensure you know what you will do after the business sells. People often end up dissatisfied with the sale if they have no plan for what to do with themselves afterward. So the goal is to help people transition. We want the buyers and the sellers to be in a good position, so everybody wins.

What if a business owner wants to get started but has no time?

--- ⊼ ---

Mike Sedlak: Being short on time is a situation many business owners face. I suggest meeting with a credentialed firm like ours to develop your "big picture" plan. This takes a few hours of your time and is not expensive. The benefits are twofold. First, once you have a framework, you can chip away at the plan over a period of time. Your plan will help keep your efforts organized. Second, you can identify any big holes in the plan while there is still time to address them.

What are examples of "holes" in people's plans?

--- ⬥ ---

Mike Sedlak: By far and away, the biggest hole in business owners' plans is that the value of the business is based more on wishful thinking than on an accredited business valuation. When the value of people's biggest asset is not known (or worse, highly inflated), any financial projection would be inaccurate. Unless you know your resources, you can't plan for retirement, buy a dream home, travel around the world, or make major gifts to family, friends, or causes. You need to know how much money you have to plan your future.

Another hole we see is that business owners overlook ways to improve the value of their business. Our process can help with this. We work with experts to identify key drivers of value and determine where the greatest opportunities lie. It is not rocket science, but it requires a disciplined approach to looking at a business objectively. If you spend all of your time working "in" the business and none of your time working "on" the business, you can miss these opportunities.

What is your favorite success story?

Mike Sedlak: We helped a business owner sell her company for a life-changing amount of money. She and her adult children got a major influx of cash. She created a fund to put her six grandchildren through college. Working with the CPA and estate planning attorney, we made sure the sale was tax efficient for income tax and estate tax by using a trust structure. Everything fell into place – but only after hard work and careful planning.

What is your role in the exit planning process?

Mike Sedlak: Exiting a business is a team sport. Sometimes we drive the process, and sometimes we fill a niche role in financial planning and investing the proceeds. When we drive the process, we start with the goals and high-level plans of the business owner. We coordinate the business valuation, develop the financial projection, work with experts to identify key drivers of value that might need attention, work with an estate planning attorney and create a plan for investing the proceeds of the sale. Our specialty and the focus of Golden Trail Advisers is on investing the proceeds. There are horror stories about people who receive large amounts of cash and invest it poorly. We help avoid that.

What don't you do?

---✦---

Mike Sedlak: We do not fix broken companies. We do not delve into marketing or operational problems. We do not restructure balance sheets. We do not resolve human resources issues. Also, we do not draft legal documents. However, we can assist in bringing the right experts to the team through our local relationships and other members of the Exit Planning Institute. We enjoy helping business owners through all of our resources.

Mike, what inspired you to get started in this field?

---✦---

Mike Sedlak: Business owners tend to be among our wealthier clients. We wanted to ensure we could help them with their financial planning and investments. I wanted to be a good resource for helping people who usually sell a business only once. I knew I needed a solid education, so I contacted the Exit Planning Institute and went through their extensive credentialing and training program. I've made many connections through the CEPA program (Certified Exit Planning Advisor). I have people who can do business valuations, help with business growth, perform transactions, and find buyers. Though my primary business is financial planning and investing, I wanted to bring all of these people to the table to address the business owner's needs in a coordinated manner.

Is there anything else you would like to share with business owners considering an exit?

———————⚡———————

Mike Sedlak: When business owners hear the term "exit planning," they often think it's not for them because they aren't considering an exit currently. However, if you dedicate just a small portion of your time and mindset toward a positive exit, you will know when the time is right to get more active in it. The more you think about it and realize it will inevitably be part of your future, the better prepared you will be. Take some time now and do some high-level planning. That will help you focus on building your company's value. One of my favorite ideas is that you can work on your business and make it better - then choose not to sell. You end up owning a better business that is more fun to manage.

How can people find you, connect
with you, and learn more?

Mike Sedlak: My email is mikes@golden-trail.com. You can also give us a call at 630-323-1111.

MIKE SEDLAK, CFP®, CFA, CEPA

FOUNDER
GOLDEN TRAIL ADVISERS, LLC

Mike Sedlak is the founder and managing member of Golden Trail Advisers, LLC. He advises business owners, executives, and individuals on financial planning and investments. Mike serves as Chief Investment Officer, responsible for client investment portfolios. Mike is a co-founder and member of a group of independent financial advisers who develop solutions for current financial issues and new regulations.

Education and Certifications

Mike has an MBA from Northwestern's Kellogg Graduate School of Management. He holds financial designations such as Certified Financial Planner (CFP®), Chartered Financial Analyst (CFA), and Certified Exit Planning Advisor (CEPA). Mike earned the designation for exit planning to better assist business owners in planning to sell their companies. Mike is a founding member of a business mastermind group that develops and shares best practices with member companies.

Complex Financial Situations

For more than 20 years, Mike has helped clients navigate complex financial matters. He helps clients grow their wealth, uncover estate planning opportunities, implement long-term financial projections, design private company retirement plans, weigh important tax considerations and plan for the financial well-being of future generations. One specialty is guiding clients through the process of enhancing the value and selling their business at a fair price. Structured properly, the sale of a business can benefit the financial future of the business owners, their families, and future generations.

Community Involvement and Family

···———————🔱———————···

Mike has held top leadership positions in organizations including the Rotary Club of Hinsdale (President, Vice President, and Board Member), St. Francis of Assisi Church (Retreat Coordinator), PADS (overnight shift supervisor), Knights of Columbus (Golf Outing Chairman) and YMCA (head of Southwest Adventure Guides). Mike and his wife live in suburban Chicago. Mike has two adult children who live in Chicago and Los Angeles. Mike enjoys golfing, hiking, boating, and being outside in nature.

EMAIL:
Mikes@Golden-Trail.com

PHONE:
630-323-1111

WEBSITE:
www.Golden-Trail.com

JAYNE
MCQUILLAN

CONVERSATION WITH JAYNE MCQUILLAN

Jayne, you are the founder of Journey Consulting, LLC. Tell us about your work and the people you help.

--- ⚜ ---

Jayne McQuillan: Journey Consulting was founded in 2007 to help business owners strategically grow the value of their business and accomplish a successful exit. We work with family-owned and privately held businesses from $3 million to $30 million in revenue. Those are our typical clients, but as with most consultants, we have some on either side of that range. We are industry agnostic and focus on business-to-business clients versus business-to-consumer. Our services include exit and transition planning, strategic planning, financial budgeting and planning, process improvement, organizational and leadership development – everything a business owner needs to exit on their terms and enjoy the next phase of life.

How much thought do business owners
put into exit planning?

- - - ——————⟰—————— - - -

Jayne McQuillan: Most business owners do minimal to no planning. In fact, statistics show that 74% of business owners have not completed any education related to transitioning a business, and 43% have done no planning at all. They also don't spend time thinking about what happens after they exit their business. Very few people like to talk about death and money, and planning for a business exit, for many, means thinking about the next stage of life.

Most business owners have no idea where to start with exit planning. The topic may seem overwhelming as they speak to their CPA, wealth advisor, or attorney. It feels complex, making it difficult to know where to begin to create a simplified process. This is where a certified exit planning advisor can come along-side the business owner and guide them through the process.

Statistics show that 80% of businesses that go to
market never sell. What are the reasons for this?

- - - ——————⟰—————— - - -

Jayne McQuillan: One of the biggest reasons businesses don't sell is owners have unrealistic expectations of the value of their business. Statistics show that less than 15% of business owners have had a valuation within the last two years. Therefore, they don't know what the business is worth. The business owner often identifies value based on blood, sweat, tears, or what their friend got for their business, but that is not how a buyer determines value. Since so much of their time and energy has gone into the business, they think it must be worth more.

The other reason is not planning for what's next. Many times, the business defines an owner's identity. They haven't asked themselves, "What am I running to?" regarding the next chapter of their lives. Planning a wedding takes up to two years to prepare for one day. When planning for the next chapter after exiting the business, most business owners do little to no planning. Yet, it's one of the largest transactions financially and personally, they will ever do.

The business owner may be burned out when they decide to sell but don't know what will fill the void of being the decision maker, the business owner, and having the day-to-day structure of being engaged in the business 24/7. Many business owners get to the table and, at the last minute, decide they aren't going to pull the trigger. Fear of the unknown is scarier than continuing to do the same thing, even though the same thing is no longer fun.

What is the role of an exit planning advisor?
How do you help business owners?

Jayne McQuillan: Exit planning advisors are certified and trained in working with business owners to position them for an exit. Our role is to help guide business owners through a systematic process to prepare their business and themselves for an exit, ensuring they know all their options. We partner with their other advisors, including their CPA, wealth advisor, and estate planning attorney, to ensure that aspects of the transition are aligned. We want to make sure we're all moving in the same direction. No single advisor has all the answers, but collectively, we can achieve the business and personal goals of the owner.

Since planning for an exit is a process, not an event, we first focus on educating business owners about the exit planning process. We offer educational seminars and training that teach them about the process and how to position themselves and their business for transition. One of the things that makes it so scary for most business owners is the confidentiality of the process. Business owners fear employees, customers, and competitors knowing they are planning to exit.

Confidentiality is critical; however, when you start well in advance of an exit, it becomes a good business strategy to plan, prepare, and execute on building value in your business every day.

Once we've engaged a business owner, we do an exit planning assessment focused on the business readiness, exit readiness, and personal and financial readiness. This includes interviews of the owner(s) and spouse(s) and key family members who may be part of the decision process. In addition, we will perform an initial estimate of business value to determine the gap between the desired value and the current value. We use this as the baseline to determine the action plans around building value in the business and positioning the owner personally and financially for an exit.

The most challenging part for most business owners is taking that first step in contacting an exit planning advisor to start the process. They don't know what they don't know. That's why we provide educational opportunities to learn about exit planning before taking that next step.

We break the process of planning and preparing for an exit into manageable chunks that work the business and business owner towards increased business value and personal readiness to provide as many options as possible to exit the business.

Jayne, what inspired you to get started in this field?

--- ———⯅——— ---

Jayne McQuillan: I started Journey Consulting 15 years ago. I'm a CPA by education and training. I'm not a tax accountant, so don't ask me for tax advice! I've worked with privately held and family-owned businesses my entire career. Out of college, I was with a large public accounting firm. I had the opportunity to be part of the mergers and acquisitions team helping business owners execute on sale transactions. I discovered I had a passion for business and specifically small to midsize businesses. I then went on to serve in executive roles in both family-owned and privately held companies.

One of my last "real jobs," as I like to call it, was with a 100-year-old family business. In addition, I was a part-time organizational development consultant with another consulting firm, working with a business owned by two families. The business was struggling immensely. In fact, they were an $8 million business losing a million dollars on the bottom line. In one of our sessions, I pulled the owner aside and said, "It's great that we're helping you with organizational development, but if you don't have a business tomorrow, it really doesn't matter." To make a long story short, this launched Journey Consulting. My passion for helping business owners achieve business and personal success drives me daily. Holistically addressing the needs of small to midsize business owners is not only good for the business owner, but it's also good for employees, customers, suppliers, and the communities in which they operate. My passion for people and business is life-long.

Is there anything else you would like to share with business owners considering an exit?

Jayne McQuillan: When it comes to exit planning, the key is to start early. Focus on how you want to build value within your business instead of the exit transaction itself. The transaction is the easy part. The real goal of exit planning is to position you and your business to exit, regardless of timing. Nobody has a crystal ball to determine when your exit will be and whether or not it will be on your terms. Our goal is to help get you and your business ready regardless of timing, including your financial plan and your next chapter, so that you have as many choices as possible to exit your business. You've spent your career building the business. You deserve to enjoy your accomplishments! We want to help you get there!

*How can people find you, connect
with you, and learn more?*

Jayne McQuillan: To get started, take our exit readiness PRE-Score at www.journeyconsult.com. You can also email us at info@journeyconsult.com to schedule a free consultation. Follow Journey Consulting on LinkedIn for regular insights you can use to build value as a business owner!

JAYNE MCQUILLAN, CPA, MBA, CEPA

FOUNDER
JOURNEY CONSULTING, LLC

A STRATEGIC MANAGEMENT CONSULTING
FIRM FOCUSED ON HELPING BUSINESS OWNERS
LIVE AN ACCOMPLISHED LIFE BY BUILDING
AND EXITING A TRANSFERABLE BUSINESS.

Combining her passion for business with her passion for people, Jayne McQuillan founded Journey Consulting in 2007 with one mission – to Change Lives by Transforming

Businesses. Her firm (stands out) by utilizing a holistic approach that engages the business, financial and personal, to achieve strategic outcomes for family-owned and privately held businesses.

Located in the heart of Green Bay, WI, Journey Consulting provides owners and their businesses with strategic planning, exit/transition planning, process improvement, and financial expertise with a focus on helping businesses build value to make exit timing irrelevant. Consultants partner with business owners to implement solid strategy and process into building value in the business while helping the business owner plan for their next chapter personally and financially.

With a commitment to educating and equipping business owners and their teams, Journey Consulting also offers exclusive training, including Value Creation Owner Roundtables, Financial Acumen Training, Process Improvement Workshops, and CEO Roundtable.

Prior to starting Journey Consulting, Jayne served in various executive roles in privately owned and family-held businesses and as an M&A advisor for a large public accounting firm. A CPA, MBA, and Certified Exit Planning Advisor, she has 30+ years of expertise in succession and transition planning, strategic planning, organizational development, budgeting, business planning, and leadership development.

To learn more about Journey Consulting, explore services and read the monthly blog, visit: www.journeyconsult.com and connect on LinkedIn.

EMAIL:
jmcquillan@journeyconsult.com

PHONE:
920-770-4141

WEBSITE:
www.journeyconsult.com

JOY RANDELS

Conversation With Joy Randels

Joy, you are the founder of The Prowess Group. Tell us about your work and the people you help.

---※---

Joy Randels: I primarily work with founders of companies. I'm a serial entrepreneur, and I've exited ten businesses successfully, had two abysmal failures, and had a couple of IPOs. Along with my team, I now work with other founders to help them grow and scale to get the highest valuation possible which is a substantial part of exit planning. In this way, they can exit when they want for the price they want.

Our framework builds on practical skills developed through 25+ years of experience as CEOs building highly successful companies and leading through challenging transitions, public offerings, mergers, and acquisitions. We have worked with over 500 CEOs, and our methodologies continue to break new ground and produce exceptional results.

How much thought do business owners put into exit planning?

···————⊼————···

Joy Randels: Many people assume if they build a business and it is generating profit, they will magically be able to exit whenever they're ready and have a nice, big nest egg for retirement. That's rarely the case unless they plan and do some work to ensure that it provides value to the next owner.

People tend to put off planning because they always think they will have time and because the business is part of their identity. When you build a business from the ground up, it becomes your baby, and you love it. The assumption is the next person who steps in will love it the same way. Whether the new owner is their child, another family member, an employee, a strategic acquirer, or a private equity firm, they rarely share the same sentiment. This is why planning for the eventual exit is so important.

What are some pitfalls business owners face if
they don't properly prepare for an exit?

Joy Randels: Most businesses don't exit; they shutter. Most people don't realize that over 75% of business owners do not have an exit plan. Owners may have an idea of what they want to do but have never formalized it. Without a clearly defined exit strategy for them and their company, you run the risk of under or overvaluing their business, paying excessive taxes, not achieving their personal objectives, and being unable to control the timing of their exit.

Most of the time, the company's value makes up a considerable portion of the owner's total wealth, but they are unaware of its actual market value. We find that, on average, most of a business owner's money is trapped inside their business, which requires planning to harvest and provide the wealth they need to achieve their long-term goals.

When owners wait to plan only, they often realize the business doesn't provide the value they need to fund their next chapter. The amount of money required to support their personal financial goals, less their net worth, less the value of the business, is what we refer to as the "wealth gap." Knowing this number is crucial because it enables us to calculate the lowest price at which the company can be sold and meet the owner's financial objectives.

Owners must also consider the "4 Cs" (human capital, structural capital, social capital, and their customers). These are valuable assets, and business owners should recognize the actual value of tangible and intangible assets. These factors are vital to understanding the business and putting processes in place so a new owner can step in and have a smooth transition.

It can also go the other way. I'm working with an owner who wants his employees to exit with him. He has a core team of six who have worked as key employees as he built the business valued at $30 million. He wants to ensure they will all have the opportunity to transition to a comfortable retirement. We helped create a transition plan that includes hiring and training all their successors so that the new owner will have a competent team from day one.

What factors determine the value of a company?

--- ——————⚓—————— ---

Joy Randels: The value of a business often depends on the buyer, especially for strategic acquirers. There are general ranges of value for companies based on the industry, financials, sustainability, and transferability. As a business owner, to exit for the maximum price, you must provide maximum value to the prospective buyers.

Your company's valuation is dynamic and regularly changes depending on your company's financial health and the state of the capital markets. Some business owners want to build large businesses, and others are happier creating a profitable small business that supports the lifestyle they want.

How does Prowess Group work with owners who decide to scale their business?

Joy Randels: Growing a business is challenging. Each step adds complexity to people, leadership, infrastructure, and market dynamics. Only 4% of the 28 million new businesses launched annually in the United States achieve $1 million in revenue. Only one out of every ten people in that group, or roughly 450,000 people, will reach $10 million; less than 17,000 surpass $50 million, and 2,500 people reach $500 million.

As founders ourselves, we have beaten those odds, not once but multiple times, with two IPOs and numerous successful exits totaling over $4 billion. During our initial conversation, we identify the owners' objectives and organizational demands allowing us to collaborate and establish precise growth goals. We can give owners the abilities, perspectives, and resources they need to turn unpredictable, complex events into opportunities. The objective is to enhance the leader's capacity to carry out the strategy, create alignment, and boost performance and productivity to support the business's expansion. We recognize that each situation is unique and leverage our experience to help our clients with those aspirations.

Does exit planning differ for small businesses versus medium or large businesses?

Joy Randels: Value acceleration is a process, not an event. It is a continual process used by company management to create value, reduce business risk, and run the business daily as though it may be sold or transferred at any time. The best part about this approach is that it can and should be used early in developing your company because savvy exit planning is an excellent business strategy. All businesses exit either by choice or due to an event. Because the process of Value Acceleration becomes a part of your everyday business operations, you can continue until you decide to sell, whether in a year or 20. By using this strategy, owners are in control and creating real wealth that can be harvested along the way while ensuring optimal value for their business when they exit.

Is there a standard plan format for creating an exit plan?

Joy Randels: There are methodologies we leverage, but every business and owner is unique, and so are their plans. Core exit planning methodologies begin with the triggering event phase of the Value Acceleration Methodology™ comprised of a business valuation and personal financial plan. We can determine their wealth, profit, and value gap from this point. We combine these core methodologies with our proprietary framework to build a comprehensive plan.

The Profit Gap is the gap between the EBITDA of your business and the industry's average and best-in-class EBITDA. The Value Gap is the difference between the multiple your business would receive if EBITDA were Average or Best-in-Class and the multiple its valuation is predicated on.

Using the Profit Gap and Value Gap, we can project the company's future rise in valuation and what it may be worth if you, the owner, choose to raise the valuation. This combination of gap assessments, market and industry data, and the owner's timeline for exit allow us to present owners with a comprehensive plan to achieve their goals.

When is the right time to start exit planning?

Joy Randels: It depends. If you've done a great job and prepared for your exit from the start, it could shorten your preparation time to perhaps six months to a year. If you haven't laid the groundwork or need to build additional value in your business to exit at the optimal time to secure the best price for your business, it could be two to five years.

One owner I'm working with is 34 years old. He and his wife are expecting their first child, and he doesn't plan to sell his company until he's around 50. His goal is to sell his business for a price that provides enough money for him and his wife to enjoy a very comfortable retirement and the ability to travel four to six months each year. They want to leave a nice nest egg for their children and future grandchildren and money for their favorite charity. To ensure they can accomplish their goals, we assembled a team of specialists to cover the areas of estate planning, wealth management, and systems to grow and maximize the value of their business year after year. We don't run the business for him; once the initial work is complete and systems are in place, we have "check-ins" to ensure everything is on track to achieve his goals. As a value advisor, I help him leverage the team he has in place and add members or remove them if needed. I started by checking in with him every 90 days, and now it's more like every six months, and we meet with the owner and his team for a few hours. We discuss where they are and what the company would sell for today. The point is, if he decided to sell his company tomorrow or had a catastrophic event forcing him to sell, it's ready to go. He would get the optimum price for the business, regardless of when he decides to sell.

Joy, what inspired you to get started in this field?

---✦---

Joy Randels: I've founded and successfully exited twelve of my own companies in the technology, professional services, business services, logistics, and transportation industries. The majority were in the technology space. Amazon acquired one company I invested in and sat on their board which sounds great, but they received pennies on the dollar of what the company was worth. There were a couple of factors that played into that. The founders were highly qualified black professionals with a female CEO. Unfortunately, women and people of color receive much less venture capital regardless of qualifications. I understand some of those challenges as a Native American and Irish female who has raised over $350M in venture capital.

When I got the call from the CEO letting me know they had agreed on terms, I thought, "Wow, this company could have been a billion-dollar company." I started examining why they had such difficulty raising the capital to scale and ultimately be acquired for a much higher multiple. I had recently exited one of my companies and was considering what to do next. I thought, "I could build another tech company or a company to help other founders grow, scale, and exit their companies." I have worked with founders while building my other companies, investing and advising them for 20+ years. So I decided to do it full-time to impact thousands of lives.

I felt the best way that I could change the landscape to make businesses, private equity, the venture capital world, and boardrooms more accurately represent our population is to work with those founders and help them grow and scale their businesses. We can create an even more significant impact by helping these founders and owners achieve the best exits. They become investors in the next generation of companies, serve on boards, and 96% of entrepreneurs donate philanthropically. The vast majority of the money that goes into philanthropy is from individual entrepreneurs, not big corporations. For me, this was the way to make the best impact I could on society. We have already worked with over 500 CEOs, and although I can't say for sure it will have the biggest impact, I think it'll be the best.

Is there anything else you would like to share with business owners considering an exit?

Joy Randels: Business owners must understand where their business is today by talking to an exit planning advisor and at least going through the initial assessment to find out where the gaps in the business are that can be improved to make it as valuable as possible.

Finding the best buyer for the owner and their business requires careful consideration. The "perfect exit" and how that vision aligns with prospective buyers and their "ideal entry" play a significant role. There are a variety of options a business owner has to exit their company, including selling (divesting) or transferring to family members, selling to their employees (ESOP), selling to private investors, or even conducting an initial public offering (IPO). However, statistics show that 90% of business owners sell to an outside third party. The best choice for a business owner depends on their objectives, financial demands, age, the state of their industry, and the state of the M&A market at the time of exit, and all play a role in which option is ideal.

Owners typically value their business at a higher price than the market, so it's imperative to have an accurate number for planning with a wealth advisor. Is it enough money to live the life you want after the business? Do you want to buy another business? Do you want to retire with your spouse? Do you want to leave a legacy in your community? What are your goals? Everyone's goals are a little bit different. That means understanding what you can and can't accomplish is essential with your accumulated wealth and the proceeds from selling your business. Then you decide the best time to exit and reap the rewards of your life's work.

How can people find you, connect with you, and learn more?

--- ⚲ ---

Joy Randels: Our website is www.theprowessgroup.com. You can reach me via email at: joy@theprowessgroup.com.

JOY RANDELS, CEPA, CIPP, CISM, ICF & WCF MASTER BUSINESS COACH

CEO
THE PROWESS GROUP

Joy launched the first of 14 ventures at age 17. Nine successful acquisitions and two IPOs later, she exercises her passion for building high-value, scalable businesses as the founder and Chairwoman of New Market Partners, where she has helped launch and fund 96 companies. Joy's most recent venture, The Prowess Group, assists founders in building valuable companies and has worked with over 1000 founders to amplify their leadership, build scalable businesses, transform valuations, and experience highly successful exits.

Having successfully climbed the corporate ladder and achieved entrepreneurial success, she claimed her spot on several public and private board directors. She proved she could win at the VC game, establishing her own fund and as a limited partner in two prominent venture funds. Joy is one of the few women to shatter the glass ceiling and claim her spot at the helm and in the boardroom.

Joy has led public and private companies from bootstrap through venture and IPO, raising over $360M in capital and generating more than $15B in revenue. She has played key roles in the design and development of software and professional service offerings for 20 years with the foremost companies in the world. As a C-level executive, her experience extends to industry leaders Apple, Akamai, and CA Technologies, where she was responsible for over $2B in revenue per year and 17 acquisitions. Joy has also founded and successfully exited businesses in the supply chain, food service, logistics, professional, and business service industries.

An alumnus of the University of Georgia, Emory University, and MIT, Joy also holds multiple board of directors, cyberse-curity, and technical certifications. A global public speaker, published author, and frequent Forbes, Fortune, and Wired columnist, Joy is a member of the International Women's Forum and UN Women's Council. Her honors include the Top 50 Women in Tech, Top Women in Venture Capital, the Florida 500, and Tampa Bay Top 100 for seven years, Florida Technology Leader of the Year, Business Woman of the Year, E&Y Entrepreneur of the Year, and numerous other awards.

EMAIL:
joy@theprowessgroup.com

WEBSITE:
www.theprowessgroup.com

LINKEDIN:
https://www.linkedin.com/in/joyrandels

LINDA RUFFENACH

Conversation With Linda Ruffenach

Linda, you are the founder of Execuity Value Advisors. Tell us about your work and the people you help.

---⚔---

Linda Ruffenach: A few years ago, I discovered my purpose, to utilize my gifts, experience, and knowledge to guide current and future business owners to see the possibilities in front of them, inspire and articulate their vision, overcome roadblocks, and maximize their potential. Today I work with business owners at varying stages of transition, from startup to exit. It could be helping figure out how to grow and scale. Perhaps they have been in business a few years and are looking at their options for pivoting or exiting. I work with them to identify where they are today and build a roadmap for how to transition with a balance between financial, business, and personal objectives. The personal piece is a key part of the equation regarding exit planning.

Are there preconceived notions about exit planning?

Linda Ruffenach: The term "exit planning" is funny because it feels like a finality. I like to use the word "transition" because it's less about "ending" and more about pivoting between the different stages of exiting your career and moving to the next chapter of your life. I always say that success can be scarier than failure, so you need to know how to handle the success, exit your business, and what that will mean to you personally and professionally. How will you achieve your goals? At the end of the day, you may not take the best price for your business if it compromises the values you held true to in building the business over the years.

I've found that business owners don't have enough information available to them about how to transition their business. That lack of knowledge and experience destroys their confidence. So they become highly unsure. Part of my role is to educate them about their options and what will ultimately be meaningful to them.

Can you give us a 10,000-foot view of
what it looks like to work with you?

Linda Ruffenach: I'll share my process. The first thing I do is look at the current state of the business. Where are you today? What's the value of your business? Do you have all the right documents in place to protect your legacy? In the first several weeks, I dig deep to understand the leadership team, history, culture, and best customers. When I refer to "best customers," I don't necessarily mean the customers with the highest revenue, even though that is very important. I am talking about the ones who fit culturally within your business. The ones that not only generate the most profits but are fun to work with and truly see value in your products and services. When you identify who they are, a company can better target the right customers. It also becomes very important when you begin looking for potential strategic buyers.

Are you positioning your company correctly? For example, one company I worked with positioned itself as a service organization, but when you dug deeper, it was really a technology company. If they had gone to market with a service-type solution, they would get a much lower multiple; instead, their valuation almost doubled. This is where we begin to outline the "story" for the business and identify the strategies that strengthen its position in the marketplace. We educate and inform the owner and create a roadmap to shore up the business, clean up financials and credentialize the story.

It's always important to really understand your financials to get the highest price possible. You need to know where and how you make money. Identifying expenses that will go away after the sale or are one-time extraordinary expenditures is key. This highly influences the purchase price. Understand and measure key financial ratios that influence value. An owner wants to get ahead of the game by looking at where they need to shore up performance in the next couple of years to increase value.

Along with accessing your business, I ask many questions about where you are, as an owner, when planning for your next chapter. 3 out of 4 business owners profoundly regret selling their business one year later. There are two main drivers. One, they did not get the money they thought they would get from the transaction. They did not calculate the cost of taxes and fees ahead of time and may have had an overinflated view of the value of the business. Business owners must understand the value of their business earlier in the process and have thought about the tax implications.

The second reason owners regret selling their business is that they did not plan enough for their next chapter. Transitioning from a position you have been in for many years to doing nothing is a major change. You can only play golf or lay on the beach so much. Having a plan for the future and your legacy is critical.

When you are ready to sell, you want to identify the right team to help you take it to the market. It may be a private transaction with a buyer already identified, or you may need to bring in a highly skilled business broker for more significant transactions in your specific industry. I have found that identifying the right investment banker or broker, who understands your industry, can help you get a much better deal and price. You also need a good transaction attorney, tax advisor, financial advisor, and a quarterback, like myself, that coordinates all the plays based on your personal, financial, and business needs.

What common mistakes do business owners make regarding exit planning?

--- ⬥ ---

Linda Ruffenach: The company I was with for 20 years was founded by ex-GE executives. So I lived in this world of discipline when it came to numbers. When I broke out and started consulting, I was shocked to find how little time business owners spent examining numbers and understanding financials. They generally look at revenue, what is in their bank account and how much they must pay in taxes. Often, their finances are built around what to do to minimize taxes versus things you want to look at when you go to market, such as bottom-line profit. This reveals that many business owners are not following a tight financial process and don't even know *how* to make money. They just know that if they sell more of this, they make more of it.

The second mistake is not having basic agreements in place. They don't have operating or buy/sell agreements, and that piece alone will create many challenges when attempting to transition. It also creates problems if something happens to the owner or one of the partners. If agreements are not in place for handling such things as death, divorce, disability, disagreement, or disaster, your business could fall apart quickly, and your legacy is no longer protected.

Third, they have not thought about the tax consequences of selling their business until it is potentially too late. Some of the same strategies used to reduce taxes along the way could lead to a large tax bill down the line. Walking through "what if" scenarios with a good tax advisor enables the owner to make the right decisions for them and their family, both short term and long term.

Linda, what inspired you to get started in this field?

--- ⟡ ---

Linda Ruffenach: Part of it was a result of personal experience. I was with a startup company that grew to over $100 million in 19 years. I was a second-generation owner, meaning the second tier of management granted ownership to help grow and maximize the final payouts. And that's precisely what I did. During that time, I went from running operations to CFO and eventually CEO, and I realized that being CEO is the loneliest role in the world. I mean, you have great players around you, support, and mentors, but it's very difficult to be candid and vulnerable in the fact that you don't have all the answers. Nobody wants to follow a CEO who doesn't know what to do. So I went out and sought guidance, and I struggled to find the kind of guidance I wanted. People either had a cookie-cutter approach of needing to follow their process or wanted to come in and take over my business. Neither one of those things worked for me.

So when I left after 19 years, I decided to fulfill a role I could never find. In that journey, I discovered the whole concept of exit planning. And I thought, "Well, that's kind of what I'm doing." It's about coaching and mentoring through those transition periods as a CEO or business owner, so it just evolved from there. I pursued additional education and got certified as an exit planning advisor and haven't looked back since. I'm having the time of my life and feel I'm in the best place in my career that I've been in a long time.

Is there anything else you would like to share with business owners considering an exit?

Linda Ruffenach: When you're making decisions about your business, stop and think about what the impact is on your clients, employees, and investors. Many business owners make impulsive decisions without considering the ripple effects down the line.

How can people find you, connect with you, and learn more?

Linda Ruffenach: You can find me on LinkedIn by searching Linda Ruffenach. My email is linda@execuity.com, and to schedule a complimentary discovery call, go to ConsultLinda.com.

LINDA RUFFENACH, CEPA

FOUNDER
EXECUITY VALUE ADVISORS

Linda Ruffenach is an entrepreneur committed to helping business owners understand and maximize the value of their business and find ways to convert that value into personal wealth. Her 20+ years of C-level experience enables her to relate to business owners' daily challenges. As the former CEO of a $100 million international enterprise, she has been through almost every stage a company can experience, from fast growth and rapid decline, to complete transformation. She has experienced firsthand how lonely it can be at the helm of an organization and what it is like to walk away from a business that has consumed much of your career.

In 2014, she founded two companies, Execuity, and Whisky Chicks. Both companies embrace the idea that knowledge and experience breed confidence, which results in empowerment. She loves to share the parallels observed between the business world and the bourbon industry and her personal stories as a female CEO, entrepreneur, author, and Certified Executive Bourbon Steward.

Linda is a skilled facilitator and has developed a systematic approach for measuring and improving the value of a business. More importantly, she knows how to turn strategy into results.

EMAIL:
linda@execuity.com

PHONE:
502.386.5504

WEBSITE:
execuity.com

OTHER:
ConsultLinda.com to schedule a complimentary discovery call

About the Publisher

Mark Imperial is a Best-Selling Author, Syndicated Business Columnist, Syndicated Radio Host, and internationally recognized Stage, Screen, and Radio Host of numerous business shows spotlighting leading experts, entrepreneurs, and business celebrities.

His passion is to discover noteworthy business owners, professionals, experts, and leaders who do great work and share their stories and secrets to their success with the world on his syndicated radio program titled "Remarkable Radio."

Mark is also the media marketing strategist and voice for some of the world's most famous brands. You can hear his voice over the airwaves weekly on Chicago radio and worldwide on iHeart Radio.

Mark is a Karate black belt; teaches Muay Thai and Kickboxing; loves Thai food, House Music, and his favorite TV shows are infomercials.

Learn more:

www.MarkImperial.com

www.BooksGrowBusiness.com

www.ingramcontent.com/pod-product-compliance
Lightning Source LLC
Chambersburg PA
CBHW071556200326
41519CB00021BB/6780